A souvenir guide

Seaton Delaval Hall
Northumberland

Jonathan Asbury

National Trust

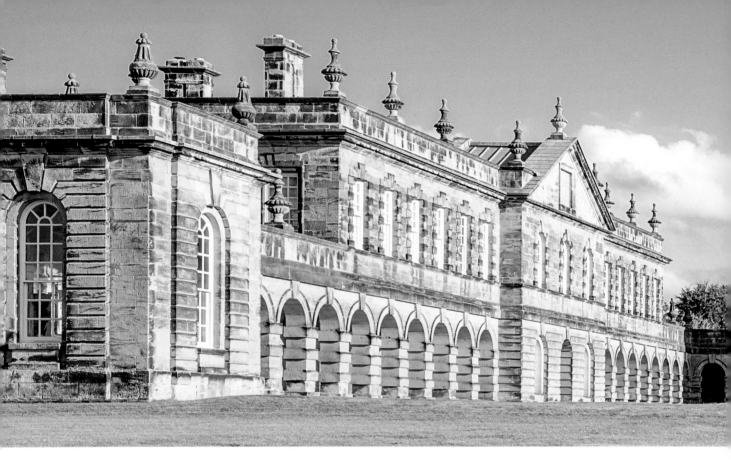

Welcome

There are so many ways to describe Seaton Delaval Hall. An architectural masterpiece. The finest house in the North East of England. The ancestral seat of ancient Norman knights. Home to a family whose name was once a byword for scandal. The scene of theatrical performances, wild parties and elaborate pranks. A charred relic. A glowering ruin. A faithfully tended survivor. A national treasure.

It is a place that defies easy categorisation. A country house like no other – with a beauty, drama and spirit that you can find nowhere else.

It is no coincidence that the National Trust allocated one of its largest ever single endowments to acquire the site in 2009, nor that this was backed up by funds raised by thousands of individual donors. This is a place that people care about. A place worth preserving.

Nor is it a coincidence that the site was identified in 2014 as the National Trust's highest priority for conservation. Its unique cultural value and poor condition – despite a lifetime of devoted care, attention and significant investment by its final family resident Lord Hastings – made an unanswerable case for urgent and dramatic intervention.

From early 2010 when conservation work first began on this latest phase of development, there has been no better place to take a look behind the scenes and witness the National Trust in action. Visitors have been welcome to explore the site, watch the Trust's experts go about their work, ask questions and see all the many ways in which the spirit as well as the fabric of the property is being restored.

Sections of the site have been closed off only to reopen with a fresh lease of life. New surprises have been planned, tales told and drama injected.

A new chapter is being written in the almost 1,000-year-old story of this remarkable place. A new scene is being set and the curtain is rising.

Welcome to the show. Welcome to Seaton Delaval Hall.

Above The East Wing and the burnt-out shell of the Central Hall

Setting the Scene

The story of Seaton Delaval Hall is one of contrasts and extremes. A tale that encompasses close to 1,000 years of riches and ruin, beauty and decay. You will encounter heroes and villains, surprises and shocks, factories and fairy lands. Industry will vie with indolence. Fame with notoriety. Fact with fiction.

It is a story that starts in the valleys of northern France and rides in conquest to the windswept coastline of Northumberland. There, over the course of centuries, you will see Norman knights become local gentry, local gentry become English noblemen, and English noblemen become figures on the national stage.

Within these generations of Delavals, some defining figures will give the story renewed impetus and direction. One is Admiral George Delaval, who in the early decades of the 18th century succeeded in rescuing the family estate from bankruptcy and commissioned the country's leading architect, Sir John Vanbrugh, to design a magnificent new house. Another is Sir Francis Blake Delaval, the eldest brother among a dozen siblings raised at Seaton Delaval Hall later that same century. So hedonistic were his tastes, so raucous his parties, so scandalous his love affairs and so great his passion for the theatrical limelight, that he propelled this extraordinary generation of the family to nationwide fame as 'The Gay Delavals'. Then too there is Sarah Hussey Delaval, niece of Sir Francis. Her own romantic dalliances with royalty saw her branded 'the wildest of her race', bringing fresh notoriety to this colourful clan.

Then a sudden twist in the tale. Disaster will strike. The family name will be extinguished, and their noble home reduced to ruins. But it will not prove to be the end of the story. Other players will emerge and play their part. A new chapter will open, and its events will unfold with every step you take around the property. We hope you enjoy the show.

Above *A View of Seaton Delaval Hall – North Front,* 1743 by Arthur Pond. Pond was appointed by the Delaval family and employed some level of artistic licence in this painting

From Normandy to Northumbria

The family name at the heart of Seaton Delaval Hall can be traced back to a castle built in the 11th century in a river valley in northern France. Known simply as 'La Val' or 'the valley', it was the focal point for a group of knights who set out in 1066 to join William Duke of Normandy, who was readying an army to fight for his claim to the throne of England. Hamo de La Val was one. Guy de La Val another, whose wife was the daughter of William's half-brother.

William, of course, became the Conqueror, the first Norman king of England, and over time his knights were rewarded with land for their service. In around 1095, it was the turn of Hubert de La Val, whose exact relationship to Hamo and Guy is unknown. King William II, son of the Conqueror, had decided to break up the old Saxon earldom of Northumbria and Hubert was granted land at Black Callerton, Dissington, Newsham and Seaton.

If Hubert were to visit Seaton Delaval Hall today, he might recognise parts of the surrounding countryside but next to nothing of the estate itself, save perhaps for one small corner. About 100 metres to the south-west of the hall lies the Church of Our Lady, some of the older sections of which were erected under Hubert's direction. He also built a small castle, which by the 13th century had become the family's main home.

Left A detail from the Bayeux Tapestry (11th century) depicting Norman cavalry carrying spears and charging the English in the Battle of Hastings

Below Originally part of the estate, the Church of Our Lady is not on National Trust land

Rise and fall

For generations the Delavals commanded respect in the region. Some served as high sheriff of Northumberland; others became border commissioners, charged with keeping the peace with Scotland. Their estate expanded alongside their business interests – especially in the production of salt and coal – so that by the early 17th century Sir Ralph Delaval was one of the richest men in the county. This same Sir Ralph turned the old castle into a mansion where, according to his son, 'he delighted much in the company of his kinsmen and friends and entertaining of strangers'. However, these were not the wild parties that would make the Delavals famous a century later. Sir Ralph 'never affected drinking' wrote his son. 'Cards nor dice he never could abide them.'

The family's upward trajectory continued when Sir Ralph's grandson (also called Ralph) was made the First Baronet of Seaton by Charles II in 1690, while his son the Second Baronet (yet another Ralph) made a good marriage to Diana, daughter of Lord Delamere. It is extraordinary, therefore, that the Delavals almost contrived to lose their property over the next couple of decades. A downturn in the estate's finances meant that the family was unable to pay a legally contracted dowry of £8,000 for the marriage of Ralph and Diana's daughter. The case went to court, bankruptcy beckoned and the estate was put up for sale.

By 1717 a buyer had been found – a rich naval man who had made a fortune out of his military and diplomatic careers – but this was not the end of over six centuries of Delaval ownership. Instead it marked the beginning of a new century of achievement, drama and notoriety for the ancient Norman line, for the buyer was Captain – soon to be Admiral – George Delaval of the Dissington branch of the family, who had grand plans for the estate and the old house at its centre.

Above Admiral George Delaval, who commissioned the hall, painted by Sir Godfrey Kneller in 1710

A home with a castle air

When Admiral George Delaval took possession of the family estate, he was approaching 50 years of age and thinking about retirement. 'I would be glad', he wrote to his brother, 'to divert myself a little in my old age in repairing the old house, making a garden and planting forest trees.'

A year later these relatively humble aspirations had been overtaken by a project of much greater ambition. Rather than repair the old mansion, the Admiral decided to build a new one, commissioning Britain's foremost architect Sir John Vanbrugh to design and carry out the work.

Work of genius

Vanbrugh had made his name on much larger commissions such as Castle Howard and Blenheim Palace, but in both cases his influence has since been diluted thanks to subsequent alterations made by other architects. His design for Seaton Delaval Hall, however, has survived largely intact, making it one of the finest examples of his genius – despite the constraints of operating to a smaller budget. In fact, it is argued that the necessarily compact nature of the design serves to intensify its impact.

Left *Sir John Vanbrugh*
attributed to Thomas Murray,
c.1719

Many features characteristic of Vanbrugh's work are there: the siting of the hall on a raised rectangular platform of land bordered by a sunken ha-ha wall; the martial grandeur of the rounded bastions at each corner of the inner pleasure grounds; the dynamic drama of the hall's towering turrets and four-floor central keep; and the playful extravagance and rich classical allusions embedded in its Baroque external decoration.

The result is at once idiosyncratic, unmistakably British and utterly in keeping with its intended occupant, the military man Admiral George Delaval. As Vanbrugh himself described one of his earliest commissions, there is 'something of the Castle Air' about the design. There is also the naval theme of the harpoons, tridents and sea creatures carved into the stonework on the north front; the sweeping views of the sea; and the overall sense of a house and gardens built for a pleasurable retirement.

It was a vision shared by both architect and patron from the outset.

'The Admiral is very Gallant in his operation, not being dispos'd to starve the design at all, so that he is like to have a very fine Dwelling.'

Vanbrugh, August 1721

Sadly, though, it was a vision that neither man was to see fully realised. Admiral George died in 1723 after a fall from his horse, and Vanbrugh followed three years later.

Much work remained to be done and it was left to the Admiral's nephew, Captain Francis Delaval, to oversee the final stages of the construction. Financing the project with money belonging to his new wife, Rhoda Apreece, heiress to the Doddington estate in Lincolnshire, he appears to have remained faithful to the spirit of Vanbrugh's intentions for the hall, and to have followed the renowned architect's principles in laying out the grounds and surrounding landscape. By about 1728 the hall was ready for Francis and Rhoda to move into, together with a young family that would eventually run to a dozen children. The scene was set, and the players were gathering for an era that would see Seaton Delaval Hall play host to the most notorious partygoers and pranksters of the age.

Above An 18th-century engraving of Blenheim Palace, another of Vanbrugh's impressive projects

Left *A View of Castle Howard*, possibly by Richard Bankes Harraden, late 18th century

An architectural masterpiece

The North front of Seaton Delaval in the County of Northumberland the Seat of Francis Delaval Esq.   design'd by Sr. John Vanbrugh Kt. 1721.

Seaton Delaval Hall has been recognised as one of the finest houses in the North East ever since its construction, and it remains perhaps the greatest – and least altered – example of the work of Sir John Vanbrugh. Its combination of large-scale dynamism, dramatic atmosphere, exquisite craftsmanship and original detail makes for a show-stopping effect that has survived even the ravages of fire, wind, rain and time.

Sir John Vanbrugh

When Admiral George Delaval was casting around for someone to design his new mansion, the name of Sir John Vanbrugh would have come up almost immediately. Indeed, it is thought that the two men may have shared a mutual friend in John Aislabie, owner of the Studley Royal Estate in North Yorkshire.

Since the turn of the century Vanbrugh had designed Castle Howard, the largest and most lavish country house of the period, and landed the plum commission to build Blenheim Palace – a reward for the Duke of Marlborough's success on the battlefield. It is astonishing then to consider that he embarked on his work at Castle Howard with no prior training or experience. Born in 1663, he had travelled to Europe and the East as a trader, spent four years as a political prisoner of the French during the Nine Years' War and joined the army before finally making a name for himself – not as an architect but as a writer of controversial and extremely successful plays.

It was in this guise that Vanbrugh met Charles Howard and there was something about this playwright – perhaps his eye for the dramatic, his well-travelled familiarity with architectural trends, or simply his reportedly 'pleasant wit and unaffected good humour' – that convinced Howard to ask him for help designing his new house. Cue another change of career, and more astonishing success for a man who would become one of the masters of the English Baroque.

Arms and the man

Vanbrugh had a profound interest in heraldry – the ancient practice of capturing a man's personal character and achievements in a coat of arms. It was a field in which he once again enjoyed great success, rising to the coveted position of Clarenceux King of Arms – an office with a history that stretches from the 14th century to the present day. It also informed his architectural work as can be seen on the north front of Seaton Delaval Hall – from the Delaval coat of arms on the gable pediment to the carvings of harpoons, sea creatures and tridents that speak to the prowess of his patron Admiral George Delaval.

The hall in its heyday

As a guest of the Delavals in the 18th century you would have alighted from your carriage in the impressively proportioned expanse of the forecourt. Then, turning away from the sweeping prospect of the sea and the Cheviots to the north you would have felt immediately taken into the embrace of the property, with the central block ahead of you and the East and West Wings to either side.

Mounting the steps to the principal floor, passing between the great columns of the North Portico, and entering the central block, you would have been greeted by the monumental scale of the Entrance Hall. Two storeys high with walls of finely carved stone, a floor of black limestone and white marble and decorated with life-size statuary, it would have quite taken your breath away.

Space for entertainment
Passing through the archway ahead and the Saloon opened out – a magnificent chamber that runs across the full width of the central block. This was the main space used for entertaining guests, with its two adjoining corner turret rooms affording a chance to sit in more intimate surroundings.

To either side of the Entrance Hall – completing the ground floor of the central block – were the Mahogany Parlour to the east and the Gilt Parlour to the west. Each had its own adjoining corner turret room, but the one next to the Mahogany Parlour was playfully concealed by wood panelling – a trick that your host would no doubt have delighted in revealing.

At either end of the central corridor that connects the Entrance Hall and the two parlours, there were oval, open-welled spiral staircases – feats of engineering rarely seen before in Britain. Each step is a single stone ingeniously fitted to its neighbours without the need for central support. Beautifully elegant, they spoke volumes for the owner's wealth, taste and attention to detail.

Heading up these stairs you would have reached two floors of rooms for family and your fellow guests. Heading down, you would find the basement, which, for all that it was primarily used by the domestic staff, was just as ambitiously conceived as the rest of the hall. Its vaulted ceilings and thick stone walls give the impression that you are in the bowels of a great castle – a sensation underlined by the fact that

Above *Seaton Delaval Hall: the North (Entrance) Front*, attributed to John Joseph Bouttats, *c.*1750

Opposite, right John Dobson's visions for Seaton Delaval Hall, created *c.*1816, were based on the original layout of the hall which included the lost South-East Wing. This wing was destroyed in the fire of 1822 and the majority of the remnants pulled down *c.*1862

Opposite, far right The Saloon in the central block, with interventions by John Dobson the corridors and chambers extend to the full width and length of the central block.

In time Seaton Delaval Hall also boasted an imposing South-East Wing – an extension almost equal in size to the adjoining central block. It provided the family with considerably more living space, including bedrooms, drawing rooms and a dining room.

The domestic facilities also extended to occupy the West Wing, with stores, laundry and servants' bedrooms sitting either side of the cavernous kitchen. As a guest you would perhaps be invited to stroll along the Long Gallery and watch the culinary preparations through a window overlooking the kitchen. You may also have been shown the East Wing, where there was originally a riding school – and a thatched building to house the horses – later converted, after around 1765, to a magnificent set of stone-stalled stables.

All the while, from almost every room and corridor, you would have caught alluring glimpses of the pleasure grounds and the surrounding landscape – whetting your appetite for further exploration. It all made for a truly remarkable backdrop for the colourful parties and entertainments for which your hosts were so well known.

'There are eight majestic fluted Corinthian columns of the most beautiful stone, and the same number of pilasters, which divide it into three spaces; the ceiling was executed by the famous Italian artist Vercelli, and is exquisitely modelled, and admirably coloured: here are several finely painted whole length pictures of this family.'

Description of the Saloon, William Hutchinson, 1778
(The reference to 'Vercelli' is thought to mean Francesco Vassalli, who had previously carried out work for Vanbrugh at Castle Howard)

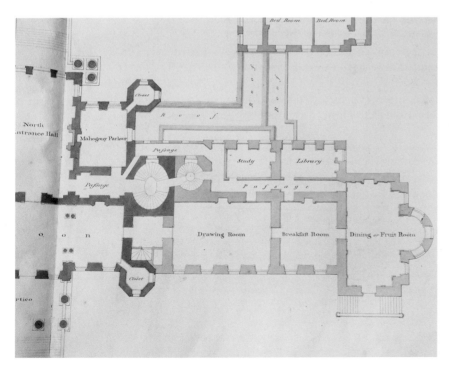

The Gay Delavals

If it was Admiral George who succeeded in keeping Seaton Delaval Hall in the family, it was his heir and nephew Captain Francis who appeared to secure the future of the Delaval line itself by fathering no fewer than eight sons and four daughters. Central to this extraordinary generation was the eldest of the eight brothers, Francis Blake Delaval. Born to inherit the riches of the estate, he was free to pursue a life of unfettered pleasure, both at Seaton Delaval Hall and in the licentious social circles of Georgian London. His antics, his passion for the theatrical limelight and his influence on his siblings soon earned the family a lasting epithet: 'The Gay Delavals'.

Francis cavorted with princes and politicians, counts and courtesans, but it was in the hedonistic company of players and playwrights that he seemed to feel most at home. Yet there was a price for this flamboyant lifestyle, and he simply couldn't afford it, running up huge debts and repeatedly having to turn to his family for help. Conspiring with a dissolute actor friend, Samuel Foote, Francis sought to solve his financial problems by tricking a rich vulnerable widow, Isabella Tufton, into marriage. Foote convinced her to visit a fortune teller, who predicted that she would meet her future husband the next day in a London park. So it came to pass, with Francis

shamelessly appearing on cue as the romantic interest, while Foote paid off the actor who had played the part of the fortune teller.

Acts of extravagance

Sadly for Francis, his new wife was nowhere near as rich as he had thought, but that didn't stop him spending a massive £1,500 of his ill-gotten wealth on a single extravagant event. Hiring the Drury Lane Theatre in 1751, he put on a performance of *Othello,* with his brothers, sisters and friends as actors. It was the talk of the town, with the House of Commons adjourning three hours early so that MPs could take their seats.

Despite, or perhaps due to, the scandalous stories attached to him, Francis remained a source of public fascination until his death at the age of 44 in 1771. Huge crowds flocked to watch his funeral cortège travel from London to Seaton Delaval Hall, where he was laid to rest in the family chapel. The Delaval name was now famous, and so too was the family home – which had played host to so many nights of bacchanalia. It was a party house without compare.

To add insult to injury for his new wife, the *Daily Advertiser* reports that the part of Emilia was played by Francis's mistress Betty Roach, with whom he lived for much of his time in London, and who bore him two illegitimate children, named Francis and Frances.

The following year, when his father died after a fall at Seaton Delaval Hall, Francis came into his inheritance. It was a responsibility for which he had no appetite or aptitude and it wasn't long before he was made to hand management of the estate over to his brother John. In return he received an annuity that predictably did not cover his expensive lifestyle, and in 1758 he decided to escape his creditors by joining the army. Extraordinarily he returned from his only military mission as a national hero, the first man to charge up the beach in a raid on St Malo during the Seven Years War. It saw Francis receive a knighthood and a measure of fame rather than his usual notoriety. It was not to last. A few years later, he was sued for 'debauching' a young and soon-to-be-famous actress.

Party house

The era of the Gay Delavals did not die with Sir Francis Blake Delaval, but it certainly began with him. In 1753, only a few months after his father's death, Francis invited 4,000 guests to enjoy an exhibition of tumbling and rope-dancing in the grounds of Seaton Delaval Hall. He is also said to have hosted boisterous evenings for the estate workers involving puppet shows, ass-racing, gurning matches, sack races, and a competition to bite off the heads of sparrows.

So wild were his parties that a disapproving visitor in the 1760s was moved to write that 'the walls and furniture are scarred to ruins by the riotous living of the scoundrel Francis, and the lust-mongers he entertains'.

That same decade, Francis installed a grand set of stables at extravagant expense and celebrated their completion with a banquet for the local gentry. When they arrived, they found the hall cloaked in darkness, apparently deserted, only for a gleeful Francis to throw open the doors of the stables to reveal a superb feast set out around the new stalls.

This was just the kind of mischief that delighted the Delavals, especially Francis and his younger sister Sarah, around both of whom all sorts of stories swirled about elaborate and often cruel jokes, tricks and wagers. Some guests retiring for the night are said to have discovered ducks and chickens in their beds; others were put to bed in a drunken stupor and woke in alarm to find themselves apparently lying on the ceiling (all the furniture, fixtures and fittings in the room had deliberately been turned upside down).

In many ways, the notoriety of the family owes as much to another Sarah – Sarah Hussey Delaval – daughter of John Delaval and niece of Francis. A noted beauty, she married an Irish peer to become Lady Tyrconnel and proceeded to court scandal by conducting barely concealed affairs, first with Prince Frederick – the second son of King George III, later to become Duke of York – and then with John Bowes, the Earl of Strathmore. Eventually she left her husband and took up residence in Strathmore's house at

Gibside in Tyne and Wear – now also a National Trust property. It was from there, after her death from consumption in 1800, that her body was transported amid lavish ceremony for burial in Westminster Abbey.

Family of performers

Francis shared his passion for theatre with his brothers and sisters, who acted alongside him in his famous production of *Othello* at the Drury Lane Theatre and in a production of *The Fair Penitent* at the Duke of York's private theatre in London. Both plays were put on by the family again some 20 years after Francis's death – this time at Seaton Delaval Hall and involving performances from members of the younger generation including Sarah Hussey.

'The theatre was erected in the hall with elegance, warmth and comfort,' wrote Henry Swinburne to a friend after a performance of *The Fair Penitent* in 1791. 'The scenery was well painted and the dresses were good. We adjourned afterwards to the Saloon, where above a hundred guests sat down to a magnificent supper, with abundance of various wines. There were some clever songs, and then dancing and card parties till the morning.'

A decade later, in 1801, an inventory of the hall mentions that props and scenery from these performances were stored at the north end of the West Wing gallery, but it is unlikely that they saw much further use as the number of surviving family members dwindled. In 1808, John Delaval died and in 1814 so too did the sole remaining brother Edward. After eight centuries of renown in Northumbria and a final century of fame across the land, the name of Delaval would no longer be held by the occupants of the ancient family home.

Opposite, above **The grand stables, created in the 1760s**

Above **Sarah Hussey Delaval, later Lady Tyrconnel, drawn by Richard Cosway**

Centre of industry

The extravagant lifestyle of the Gay Delavals – and the fortune of the family for centuries before – was based on the natural riches of their estate. The oldest industry was salt production, which began in the area at least as far back as the 14th century. It involved evaporating sea water in huge pans over coal fires and resulted in salt of such quality that it was much sought after in Elizabethan London.

Fundamental to efficient salt production was the ready availability of coal, and it was in this respect that the Delavals really struck lucky. Over the years, some 30 pits went into operation in the local area, making it a large and immensely profitable industry for the family – either directly through mining on their estate or indirectly through trade and shipping.

Coal too was one of the materials necessary for the production of glass – along with clay, sea sand, sea kelp and copperas (another by-product of the coal industry), all of which were also available in abundance. In 1763, to take advantage of these resources, the Delavals constructed the Royal Northumberland Bottle Works – the largest glassmaking factory in the UK, which by 1777 was producing some 1.74 million bottles per year.

Trading hub

The key to taking full advantage of the salt, coal and glass industries was having a port from which to trade. The Delavals were again fortunate to have a natural harbour available to them at the village of Hartley Pans at the mouth of Seaton Burn, and it is known that salt started to be shipped to market from there in 1550.

Above The Royal Northumberland Bottle Works in Seaton Sluice, c.1895

Less fortunate was the tendency of the harbour to become silted up, which meant that it was not deep enough to accommodate large ships during loading. Instead they had to wait outside the harbour while their cargo was laboriously transported out by smaller vessels. In 1660 Sir Ralph Delaval improved the facilities by adding a pier, and years later he constructed a set of sluice gates, which captured water at high tide and |then released it to wash the troublesome silt out to sea. It proved such a success that the port became known as Seaton Sluice, but it did not solve the problem entirely; at the lowest tides the harbour still became too shallow.

In the 1760s Sir John Delaval addressed this problem by cutting a new entrance to the harbour and adding sluice gates at either end to create a deep-water dock. This allowed for the export of far greater quantities of goods and saw the family prosper like never before. In 1785 the tax alone paid to the government on salt, glass and coal shipped from Seaton Sluice came to £24,000, which relative to average wages would be around £35 million today.

Above, left John Hussey Delaval (1728–1808), creator of the deep water dock at Seaton Sluice. Painting by William Bell, 1774

Above, right 'The Cut' at Seaton Sluice, looking out towards the North Sea

The great fire

Late in the afternoon on 3 January 1822, a burning ember wafted up one of the chimneys in Seaton Delaval Hall. Perhaps it met with an exposed section of beam. Perhaps it lit upon a tinderbox tangle of twigs and leaves – the desiccated detritus left by generations of nesting birds. Either way, a spark became a flame, and a flame became a fire – a fire that raged so fiercely that it was mistaken for a sunset of unusual brilliance by sailors gazing westwards from their ships near Whitley Bay.

For five long hours it blazed, as hundreds of locals battled to quell the flames and rescue what they could of the building and its contents. Panes of glass melted in the heat. Molten lead rained down from the red-hot roof. Floors collapsed.

Above, left Relics from the fire: a face in the wall of the Saloon

Above, right Only skeletons of the railings on the spiral stairs from the Basement to the Central Hall survived the fire

The East and West Wings were saved, but the central block suffered catastrophic damage. The upper storeys and roof were consumed, leaving the Entrance Hall and Saloon gaping up at the winter sky. Only the Mahogany Parlour and Tapestry Room survived in any recognisable form. Irreparably damaged too was the South-East Wing – a major extension to the hall which boasted comparable dimensions in length and height to the adjoining central block. It was here that the fire is thought to have originated and it was left in such an abject and dangerous state that workers eventually had to demolish it altogether. Seaton Delaval Hall lay in ruins.

'The fire burnt with such fury as to bid defiance to all human efforts. The glass in the windows, by the intense heat, was reduced to a liquid state and the lead in the roof poured down like water.'

Report in the *Newcastle Chronicle*, 14 January 1822

Below, left **The Central Hall**

Below, right **Molten roof lead left these stains on the walls of the Saloon**

Decay and decline

Even before the great fire of 1822, Seaton Delaval Hall had become a place where the past spoke more loudly than the future. Sir Jacob Astley (5th Baronet, 1756–1817) of Melton Constable in Norfolk had inherited the estate from his uncle, Edward Delaval. It was thought to be his son or grandson – both also Jacob (the 16th and 17th Baron Hastings respectively) – who engaged the services of Newcastle architect, John Dobson, best known now for his work on Grey Street and Newcastle railway station, to design a new South-West Wing. It is unclear if this work ever began, but if it did, it was soon abandoned when Sir Jacob died in 1817.

Below John Wykeham Archer's painting of Seaton Delaval Hall in 1858, before it was re-roofed

His son and heir, who later became the 16th Baron Hastings, does not seem to have given Seaton Delaval Hall much attention. He rarely visited his Northumberland estate, and had even less reason to do so after the hall was destroyed by fire. The once glorious central block was left exposed to the withering effects of wind, rain and ice for the next 40 years.

Tentative recovery

Hopes of a brighter future were rekindled in 1861 when the 17th Baron Hastings re-commissioned John Dobson to re-roof the hall and patch up the most badly damaged sections of the building. The extensive red brickwork now visible in the Saloon – and the installation of supporting iron columns – dates from this period. It seems likely that the intention was to reconstruct the hall entirely and renovate its interior, but both the funds and the will appear to have run out.

By this time an air of deterioration hung over the entire estate. The industries that once generated such fortunes for the Delavals were in decline – gradual at first, but then sudden and catastrophic when 204 men and boys died in an accident at the New Hartley Colliery in 1862. This led to improved safety standards in pit design – such as the mandatory use of two shafts – but it also hastened the demise of the coal-shipping industry at Seaton Sluice. Instead cargo trains were used with ever-greater frequency on the Blyth and Tyne railway to transport the coal to the Tyne for shipment. The once mighty glass industry also followed suit, with the Royal Northumberland Bottle Works forced to close its doors in 1870.

What life there was at Seaton Delaval Hall now centred around the local community, who made use of the partially maintained grounds for garden parties and cricket matches – all under the benign distant patronage of Baron Hastings.

Parish meetings were held in the Mahogany Parlour and at Christmas time the Entrance Hall was decorated with trees, lanterns and flags. This drift of the property from private to public was underlined in 1891 when Baron Hastings agreed that the Church of Our Lady – for centuries the Delaval family's private place of worship – could become the local parish church. It was a sign of things to come.

Above *Seaton Delaval Hall* by John Dobson

Below An engraving from *The Illustrated London News* of the New Hartley Pit Disaster of January 1862

VIEW OF HARTLEY COLLIERY FROM THE RAILWAY, TAKEN SHORTLY AFTER THE CATASTROPHE.

Two World Wars

Above *Seaton Delaval,
the central block, 1941* by
John Piper

When Britain entered the First World War on 4 August 1914, Lord Kitchener, the new war minister, issued an appeal for 100,000 volunteers to join the ranks of the army. By the end of September, he had 750,000. There was an especially enthusiastic response in the North East, and Seaton Delaval soon found itself as the base for 'D' Company of the 3rd Battalion, the Northumberland Volunteers. Later the Tyne Garrison, charged with defending the coast against possible German attack, set up camp in the fields surrounding the hall. Little is known about how the hall itself was used but it is thought that the army may have had access to some of the buildings given that estate workers later complained about wear and tear in the service wings.

Between 1921 and 1938 it is known that the West Wing of the hall was let as a residence for a Colonel George Pollard, his wife Maria and their young family. Decorated for his bravery in the First World War, Pollard became first mining engineer and then managing director of the Seaton Delaval Coal Company. His family's legacy can be seen today in the hall's Rose Garden, which was reinstated under their direction during this period, and later renewed by the 22nd Lady Hastings.

Terrifying plans

Ironically it was in an era of peacetime that Seaton Delaval Hall faced its most existential threat. In 1937 plans were drawn up to demolish the hall and most of the pleasure gardens and build an estate of 382 semi-detached houses. Quite why the project was not enacted is not clear, but the hall survived to be one of the many country estates requisitioned for military use during the Second World War.

It was in this guise that war artist John Piper came across what he described as 'this vast old war-horse of a house … built with a splendid sense of drama'. Thanks to a pre-war interest in derelict architectural ruins, he had been commissioned to travel the country painting bomb-damaged churches. En route, he made a stop at Seaton Delaval Hall and found himself moved to capture the drama of its colouring in his trademark oils – 'ochre and flame-licked red, pock-marked and stained in purplish umber and black'. One of the two paintings he produced is now part of the Tate Collection.

Left A fire extinguisher, with instructions in German, still sits in situ in the East Wing

Left, below Repatriation notice pinned to the back of one of the rooms in the East Wing, which was used to house prisoners of war in the Second World War

Piper described the hall as a 'barrack and store' and talked about troops using the 'gorgeous stables' as an ablution space, but later in the war it became a camp for German and Italian prisoners of war. Rooms in the East and West Wings were set aside to house the men, who were expected to rise at five in the morning, parade on the courtyard before six, and then disperse to work on local farms. After an eight-hour day of threshing wheat, picking potatoes or digging drains, it was then back to their bunks and dreams of home.

Evidence of their time on the estate still remains in closed-off sections of the East Wing, where notices written in German and Italian are pinned to the back of bunk-room doors, graffiti is etched on shutters, and window sills have been removed to feed the prisoners' habit of carving wooden toys.

Held in trust

Seaton Delaval Hall remained in military requisition until 1948, when it was returned to the stewardship of the 21st Baron Hastings. However, it was his son Edward Astley, later to become the 22nd Baron, who took it upon himself to breathe new life into the property.

It was badly needed. The basement was filled with leaves and other detritus, generations of pigeons had wrought havoc in the Entrance Hall and Saloon, rainwater was seeping through the roofing on both wings, and the structural integrity of the entire house was fast deteriorating.

Tireless champion

The future Baron Hastings was determined to reverse this decline and set about restoring the fabric of the building – re-roofing the East and West Wings and making repairs to the stables – reassembling its collections and readying it to be opened to the public. The first visitors made their way up the steps of the portico in the summer of 1950, but much work still remained to be done. Indeed, after assuming his peerage in 1956, the 22nd Baron and his wife Lady Hastings spent the rest of their days continuing to make improvements to the site, re-glazing many of the windows, restoring the South Portico and installing electricity and central heating. From 1990 onwards, they chose to live in the West Wing and remained there until 2007 when they died within months of each other. Their graves can now be found in the grounds of the Church of Our Lady, marked by a stone carrying the words, 'who together made the Hall into a home'.

Above One of the most notable additions made by the 22nd Baron Hastings and his wife to the Seaton Delaval Hall Estate was the Parterre to the north-west of the hall. Installed in the 1950s, it was designed by James Russell of Sunningdale Nurseries, who was then just starting out on a career that would later take him to Castle Howard

That same year, Delaval Astley the 23rd Baron Hastings asked the National Trust if it would consider acquiring the site. This prompted perhaps the largest public consultation ever conducted by the Trust, with over 100,000 people giving their views. The response – driven especially by the passion of the community immediately around the hall – was overwhelmingly in favour of acquisition, which was jointly supported by an extraordinary public fundraising campaign and one of the largest single endowments ever allocated by the National Trust.

On one matter everyone involved in the acquisition was agreed. Seaton Delaval Hall – with its remarkable history – was not to become 'just another country house'. Today, after a decade of meticulous analysis of the condition and significance of the entire estate, the Trust has set about underlining its commitment to this pledge.

Left Hastings Family Portrait at Seaton Delaval Hall with Bellina the dog and Bundle the cat, 1961

Silent witnesses

One early priority for the Trust was to make safe the six statues that adorn the upper arcades of the Entrance Hall. Representing the muses – for architecture, painting, music, sculpture, geography and astronomy – they were in danger of either falling apart or falling down or both. Investigations revealed that the statues had been constructed using an unusual method, with mortar, plaster and plaster-soaked cloth wrapped and formed around an iron framework. To make matters more complicated, this frame was found to be fixed into the walls, which meant that the statues would have to be restored where they stood.

Further tests, including the use of portable x-ray equipment, revealed additional fractures in the plaster and rust on the central iron frame, which helped the conservation team decide on the best plan of action. This included the first ever use of cathodic protection technology on a statue, which involves sending an electric current through the iron framework to prevent it from rusting. Previously only used to treat iron beams in old buildings, it was just one example of the expertise that would eventually be required to make Seaton Delaval Hall safe for generations to come.

You'll always find me in the stables at parties

'Sir F. B. Delaval invited a large and brilliant company to an entertainment at Seaton Delaval; the guests assembled, and waited long, and seeing no signs of preparation, began to think themselves the victims of one of Sir Francis's jokes. At last doors were thrown open, and they were ushered, not into the dining-room, but into the stable, the great vaulted hall, 62 ft. by 40, which occupies the eastern wing. Here they found all the usual stable fittings removed, and a gorgeous feast laid out in a brilliantly lighted and decorated hall.'

R. E. G. Cole writing in *History of the Manor and Township of Doddington*, 1897

Raising the Curtain

Once you are familiar with the story of Seaton Delaval Hall, its worth to the nation becomes obvious. Here we have one of the finest surviving examples of the genius of architect Sir John Vanbrugh – its artful blend of building and landscape standing in favourable comparison to his famous works at Blenheim Palace and Castle Howard.

Add to that the extraordinary exploits of the Delaval family, the rich industrial heritage of the estate and the terrible beauty of the fire-ravaged hall, and it is not hard to understand why the site is so widely treasured. It is no coincidence that thousands of people came together to donate over £1 million towards the acquisition of the site by the National Trust.

This, however, was only the first step towards building on the steadfast work of Lord Hastings to save the property. Over the next few years there followed a long and immensely detailed investigation to determine the overall condition of the site. The results were troubling. The fabric of its buildings and stonework had deteriorated to the extent that elements of Seaton Delaval Hall – with all of its wonders – stood at real risk of being lost.

This simply could not be allowed to happen and so, by 2014, this time-worn house on the windswept coast of Northumberland had become the National Trust's highest conservation priority.

Thanks to an award of £3.7 million from the National Lottery Heritage Fund, a further £3 million from the National Trust and just under £750,000 brought in through a significant programme of fundraising, the property has entered a new chapter in its life – rescuing it from further decline, adding new visitor facilities and weaving together the story of the hall and the Delavals in a way that combines the fun, energy, showmanship and mischief of this most flamboyant of families.

The planned transformation was so infused with a sense of theatre that the National Trust decided to call it the *Curtain Rises* project.

Left Staff and volunteers celebrate the award from the National Lottery Heritage Fund in the Saloon, April 2018

The National Trust at work

The sheer scale of the work included in the *Curtain Rises* project speaks volumes for the threat that Seaton Delaval Hall faced. In the hall, the basement had to be re-floored and protected from leaks and flooding, and the wonderful spiral staircases to the east and west needed to be conserved and made safe. The West Wing needed a new roof and interior repair to address areas of damp and weathering, and in the East Wing some of the magnificent stone stalls in the stables were close to collapse.

In fact, barely a building or structure of any kind on the property was not included in the planned work – whether restoring the stonework of the ha-ha and bastions, addressing issues with the brickwork of the walled garden, or making safe the Orangery and Mausoleum ahead of further possible restoration. Then too there were the new visitor facilities such as the much-improved café to be built in the Brewhouse – itself an architecturally significant building that required delicate handling – and all the work required to restore and re-imagine the pleasure gardens.

As if this were not enough, the team also had to take into account that the *Curtain Rises* project would only be the first phase of an on-going programme of development at the site. They needed to set the stage for new scenes to be performed and enjoyed, factoring in how the property could best be presented to visitors after the work was completed, and how best to bring the story and colour of the Delavals to life both inside and outside the hall.

Open house

Given the extent of the work involved, the Trust considered closing the site for the duration of the project, but instead it decided to make Seaton Delaval Hall a showcase for its work. Visitors would still be able to explore different sections of the site, and better still they would be able to see all of the various specialist teams at work, and even ask them questions. It would be a chance to get a peek behind the scenes at the broad range of expertise that goes into a project of this kind.

From the National Trust alone, for example, the planned work required contributions from specialists in landscape and nature, conservation and collections and risk management, as well as curators, archaeologists, building surveyors, estate managers, planners, gardeners and volunteers. It ranged across almost every department from finance to food, commercial to marketing, fundraising to visitor experience, and it was all conducted with input from a host of specialist advisory groups.

From outside the Trust, the list was perhaps even longer. Visitors could expect to come across paint conservators, ecologists, stone masons, timber specialists, architects, archaeologists, structural engineers, creative designers, building contractors, landscape architects, fire safety officers, mechanical and electrical engineers, play design specialists, kitchen designers, audio-visual specialists, graphic designers, hydrologists, mining engineers, health and safety officers, metal workers, arboriculturalists, geophysicists, quantity surveyors, community consultants, insurers, or representatives from official bodies such as Historic England, the Georgian Society, the Highways Commission, Northumberland County Council Parks and Gardens, and the Society for the Protection of Ancient Buildings.

Many were the hands that pulled the rope to raise the curtain on Seaton Delaval Hall.

Above **The stables**

Opposite **The spiral staircase of the Central Hall, looking up from the basement**

The architectural challenge

Jenny Gillatt is a director of Mosedale Gillatt Architects, the specialist architectural practice chosen to investigate, plan and carry out the required conservation and building work at Seaton Delaval Hall. There is no one better placed to explain the peculiar challenges and charm of this Vanbrugh masterpiece.

What were your first impressions of Seaton Delaval Hall?
It's a site that has always fascinated me. It's such a fine example of Vanbrugh's work and so monumental. The mansion just sits there and looks at you. It really lets you know it's around.

From an architect's point of view, the ha-ha and bastions are marvels of engineering, and the hall is just fabulous. It has this echoing sense of ruin – almost cathedral-like. I love the way you can see all of its scars and how it has changed over time. The whole estate is a place where your imagination can take flight. Step into the stables and you can almost hear the horses breathing and eating and shifting their weight. It's wonderful.

How did you decide what work to carry out?
With any historic structure, you don't do anything unless you really need to. The key factors are significance and risk. The National Trust had made their own assessment, and we then investigated all of the site's structures to determine what their condition was, what risks they faced, whether they could be dealt with in the short or long term, and how significant they were to the site as a whole.

What does an investigation like that involve?
To begin with, it's survey work. We spent weeks analysing and drawing every single wall in the walled garden, the stonework of the bastions, and every stone in the ha-ha, which is about 1.6km long. It's the only way to make a proper analysis of what needs doing.

The challenge then lies in striking the balance between intervening or not. It takes a lot of discussion – with Historic England, with the conservation officer, the building surveyor, the Trust, the structural engineer. And then there are all the specialists that the Trust can call on for things like paint analysis. It really is a team effort.

What were the absolute priorities?
In the hall, it was the basement. It was soaking wet and with freeze–thaw cycles the sheer dampness of the masonry was soon going to cause problems. We really needed to stop water getting in and, among other things, that meant lifting the steps leading up to the North and South Porticos, inserting a membrane, and then re-laying them. We also had to be careful not to dry the basement out too quickly, because that in itself would cause too much movement. The floor was very uneven too, so some visitors couldn't experience the space. It needed completely re-flooring and re-lighting.

Do you have to be careful about the methods you use?
Yes, when we're consolidating or repairing a structure we always use traditional materials and techniques. But if we are intervening – repurposing the Brewhouse for example to become a café – our approach is to employ the best of contemporary design and materials.

Why is that?
I feel we owe it to the original architects, because that's what they did in their time – they pushed boundaries and explored the latest tools and technologies. There's a tradition there that it's a privilege to be part of – especially at a property as wonderful as Seaton Delaval Hall.

Conservation in action

In 1752 a guest at Seaton Delaval Hall was given a tour of the gardens and later recalled coming across some stone sheep. Not that he realised they were statues at first. They were so life-like, he noted, that they 'would deceive almost anybody till very near them'. Over 250 years later, when the baton was handed to the National Trust, about half a dozen of these sheep still lay in a sorry condition scattered around the gardens – one half buried in the ground. Meanwhile, by a wall in the Rose Garden, there sat a statue of a shepherdess, also somewhat weather-beaten and crudely patched up with daubs of concrete.

Below Stone sheep, thought to date from around the time the hall was built

Struck by the similarities in style between the shepherdess and the sheep, the curators at the Trust decided to reunite the young woman with her flock and position them to offer the same kind of gently deceptive surprise described back in the 18th century.

This then became just one project among the many planned as part of the *Curtain Rises* work and, like so many others, it was reliant on the skills of the National Trust's conservation team. Neither the shepherdess nor her flock were in any fit condition to survive much longer outside. Their stonework needed careful cleaning and stabilisation; new plates had to be prepared for them to rest on; and the shepherdess in particular needed to have her concrete patches removed so that her scars and blemishes could be more sensitively repaired.

Similar projects were planned for almost every corner of the property – from rescuing the stone stalls in the stables from collapse, to treating and restoring the delicate workings of a clock found abandoned in the roof of the West Wing. Together they promised to build on decades of earlier care and attention to conserve Seaton Delaval Hall for the enjoyment of generations to come.

Sleepless nights

The decision to carry out any conservation work is based on an analysis of the often complex interplay between an object's significance, its condition, its use and the threat it faces if left untouched. This can lead to a lot of discussion, as curator Jo Moody recalls opposite.

What was the hardest conservation decision you had to make?
Without doubt the spiral staircases. When Vanbrugh put them in, he was playing with something that other architects weren't. They were really unusual for their time. That on its own makes them significant, but so does their beauty – both in their original design and in the scars they bear from the fire.

So why not leave them untouched?
They were structurally unsound and had become worn down by use over the years. We wanted visitors to continue using them to access the basement and first floor, which meant doing some work to make them safe, but the moment you do anything to improve their structural integrity you risk destroying some of their aesthetic and historic value.

How do you solve a dilemma like that?
With lots of agonising! We checked and double-checked every single step of our decision-making process to make sure that we took into account every possible factor and option. It kept me awake at night, but I think we ended up striking the right balance between what's right at this point in time and what's right for the future.

Discoveries and mysteries

Putting together a plan for the *Curtain Rises* project required an investigation of the site in far greater detail than anything previously attempted. A team of hardy volunteers cleared undergrowth from the ditches of the ha-ha, so that the wall could be closely inspected stone by stone. Paint analysis experts measured the layers of dust between coats of paint to understand when and how often they were applied. Archaeologists used pulses of laser light to search out elements of the estate's past otherwise hidden from view, and ecologists braved the elements to better understand the local flora and fauna.

It was an investigation that confirmed much that was already known about the property, but it also yielded some surprising discoveries, raised intriguing questions and left some longstanding mysteries unsolved.

Lost property

Investigations in the East Wing during the *Curtain Rises* project led to the discovery of a ring. It was hidden on a ledge above a door in rooms once occupied by German and Italian prisoners of war. Cigarette packets and a bottle of anti-gas ointment were also found under some loose floorboards in the same room.

Left Conservation work in the Old Kitchen in the West Wing revealed what is thought to be a large emblem of the Cameronians (Scottish Rifles) on the wall. It matches graffiti found elsewhere across the site and investigations are ongoing

Home to roost

Perhaps the most startling discovery was that within the nooks and crannies of the hall lay a common pipistrelle bat hibernation roost larger than any previously known in the UK. Staff and visitors had often spotted individual bats weaving and darting around the site, but it is now thought that hundreds may lurk within the walls of the hall. What made this especially surprising was that pipistrelles are usually thought to roost in cool, moist and dark locations, whereas the crevices at Seaton Delaval Hall are dry and well lit. It was a discovery that informed not only the conservation work planned as part of the *Curtain Rises*, but also the broader scientific understanding of this fascinating species.

Strange markings

While the Brewhouse was being readied for its conversion into a café, strange markings were noticed on one of the windowsills. Archaeologists believe they were made in the superstitious belief that they would protect the building and its occupants from danger. Brewing, with its need for a furnace to boil large amounts of water, was a relatively risky business, which may explain the workers' inclination for such rituals.

Abiding mysteries

Many questions remain unanswered about Seaton Delaval Hall. Stories abound, for example, of the pranks played by the Delavals – of beds being lowered into water and 'walls' suddenly being raised as guests undressed for the night – but it is not clear whether they were played here or at their other properties. Given that all the bedrooms in the hall were destroyed by the fire, it seems we will never know the answer.

Legend also has it that a 'White Lady' can sometimes be seen at one of the windows on the eastern side of the central block. She is said to be the ghost of a young woman who became engaged to Jack Delaval, the only male heir in the generation that followed the Gay Delavals. Hoping for a better match, his father Sir John sent young Jack away only for him to become ill and die. His intended bride, driven mad with grief, is believed to await his return still. Suffice it to say that hard evidence of this ghostly apparition has not yet been discovered!

Above A common pipistrelle bat, a species which has made a home at Seaton Delaval Hall

Left A fragment of a Bellarmine jug found near the Brewhouse. It dates from the mid-17th century and we think it may have been made by a group of potters called the *Rosenkrantzbruderschaft* who worked near Cologne in Germany. Bellarmine jugs were named after Cardinal Roberto Bellarmine, a 17th-century cardinal who opposed Protestantism and supported a ban on alcohol. This was a direct snub as the jugs usually contained liquor

Pride of place

The ties between Seaton Delaval Hall and the local community have always been strong. For centuries, men and women in the area have made their living under the benign patronage of the Delavals, and later the Astleys. In the heyday of the hall and grounds alone, there would have been housekeepers, stewards, maids, cooks, brewers, gardeners, grooms, stewards and general labourers on the site, and further afield the business interests of the Delavals made them responsible for many more employees in the salt, coal and glass industries.

When fire tore through the hall in 1822, it is telling that hundreds of locals flocked to try to quench the flames, risking their lives to save what they could of the building and its furnishings. Some of those same locals – and their children and grandchildren – would return to the grounds of the hall over the years to play cricket on the South Lawn and attend garden parties. They came to worship too, after the ancient Delaval family chapel became the local parish church in 1891.

People power
The survival of the hall to the present day owes a great deal to the wider community. When the National Trust first considered acquiring the property, more than 100,000 people were moved to respond to a public consultation on the decision. Many also delved deep into their pockets to help raise the funding required.

Today, many volunteers give their time to support Seaton Delaval Hall, bringing a great deal of knowledge and skill to go alongside their evident pride and passion for the property.

The *Curtain Rises* project was not conceived in isolation but together with the communities and partnerships that support the hall. Delaval Dialogues for example, which forms part of the project, is an opportunity for Seaton Delaval Hall to work creatively with the local community. Through collaboration with local schools, young people, community groups and organisations across the generations it will see the stories, significance and potential of the hall brought to life through anything from artistic performances, to allotment growing to a group for young nature protectors.

Then there is the Rising Stars programme – a partnership between Northumbria University and the National Trust at Seaton Delaval Hall. Born from a desire to provide opportunities for students to gain experience working across a range of areas in the heritage sector, it supports students to work with the National Trust on key areas such as conservation in action, innovative interpretation, programmes for schools and creative residencies.

Left Children from Seaton Sluice First School finding out more about bats on site with the hall's ecologist and landscape team, February 2019

Enjoying the Show

Seaton Delaval Hall demands attention. You don't need to know anything about Vanbrugh or the Delaval family to be captivated by its brooding presence, but enter within its bastioned perimeter and you cannot help but want to know more. Why is the house in ruins? What must it once have looked like? Who built it, and who lived here?

Discovering the answers to any of these questions then reveals further sources of fascination – the great fire of 1822, the wonder of Vanbrugh's design, and perhaps most intriguingly of all, the Gay Delavals with all of their riotous parties, scandalous antics and flamboyant theatricality.

It's only if you can connect this extraordinary history to the hall and grounds around you that the whole site comes to life. You start to picture the revellers thronging to the pleasure gardens in their thousands to watch an evening of circus entertainments; you hear the yelp of an unfortunate guest as they discover a duck lurking under the covers of their bed; and you feel the heat of the flames that so dramatically sealed the house's fate.

Over the years the connections between the hall and its stories had become all but hidden, and visitors could too easily leave without a full appreciation of the site's character. This then was the other aim at the heart of the *Curtain Rises* project – to reanimate the unruly spirit of Seaton Delaval Hall and present its stories afresh to a new generation of visitors.

Right George Orange performs at Carnival Capers, July 2018, part of the Great Northumberland festival

Questions of interpretation

To help determine how best to present the hall, the National Trust turned to visual artist and scenographer Imogen Cloët and production specialist Niall Black. Both hail from the theatre world where their task is to design and create spaces in which audiences can really engage with a play or performance. As Imogen explains, they employ the same techniques to help visitors understand and appreciate historical sites – a process referred to as 'creative interpretation'.

How would you describe your work?

It's about creating immersive, multilayered environments that surprise and intrigue. That's something Niall and I have done in theatre for over 25 years, and in heritage spaces for the past ten years for organisations including English Heritage and the National Trust.

Where do you start?

By spending time on site immersing ourselves in the building and the collection and by talking to staff and volunteers. They know the place so well, and they all have their own take on the building and its stories. Then it's all about research – finding out as much as possible about the stories and people related to the property. All too often a visitor will see a portrait but not the person in it. We need to bring those people to life somehow. These are the characters in the story.

What did that process reveal to you about Seaton Delaval Hall?

Well, after some public consultation, the Trust decided the period they wanted the two of us to focus on was from when Vanbrugh was commissioned to build the hall by Admiral Delaval through to the death of the Delaval family name and the fire of 1822. But even within that relatively narrow time frame, there are so many stories to tell. It is an exciting commission because the Trust has given us an opportunity to do something new and dynamic.

In what way?

Many properties come with a large collection of the furniture and works of art that adorned the place in its prime. All of that often has to be preserved in situ, which limits what you can do in terms of presentation. With Seaton Delaval Hall, because of the fire, there are relatively few pieces that date from the period of the Delavals. Most of the collection was brought in much later. That gives us much more leeway to move things around, really focus in on the stories of the few surviving items and take some risks when creating an experience for the visitors.

Tell us about that experience. What did you want to create?

A sense of drama and mischief. The Delavals loved throwing parties and putting on productions. There was a definite theatricality to all their pranks and they loved having an audience. I don't think guests ever knew what to expect when they visited the hall. Because there are so few physical traces left of the family in the building, we felt that this sense of energy and mischief had been lost. Vanbrugh's incredible hall was like a fantastic stage set but without a show.

So visitors can expect to be entertained?

Yes, and informed. We wanted to strike a balance between telling the outrageous stories about the Delavals and exploring the early Georgian society they lived in and how they came to have such wealth and status. So visitors will discover industry as well as revelry, trade as well as pranks, and art as well as drama. It will be fun and playful. They can expect the unexpected.

Plays and performances

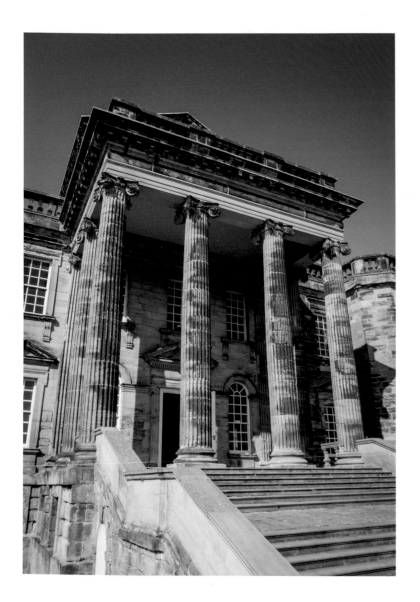

The Gay Delavals were united by a love for theatre. Francis, John, Thomas, Anne and Sarah all trod the boards together in various combinations – both in London and at their Northumbrian home – and as a child their brother Robert is said to have entertained guests to the house with a seasonal pantomime.

It is all too easy to imagine such performances being staged in the great Entrance Hall at Seaton Delaval Hall – the audience seated to face the action, the corridor running from east to west acting as the wings, and perhaps the upper balcony corridor affording additional dramatic possibilities.

When Francis and his siblings were growing up, theatrical performances followed the Baroque tradition – characterised by the use of elaborately painted scenery and ingenious mechanisms to bring movement, sound effects and the illusion of perspective to the performance, all framed as if in a painting by a noble proscenium arch.

This same tradition of Baroque theatre was the chief inspiration for the way the *Curtain Rises* team planned to transform the presentation of the hall and gardens. Walking around the site would become an experience filled with colour, illusion, surprises and carefully framed tableaux. Think props and scenery, sound effects and peepholes, stagecraft and drama.

Left From the south, the hall's portico entrance resembles those of theatres such as Newcastle's Theatre Royal and London's Drury Lane

David Garrick as John Brute in Vanbrugh's the 'Provok'd Wife', Drury Lane, *c.*1763. Painting by Johann Zoffany

Parties, pleasure and pranks

If you had visited Seaton Delaval Hall in the era of the Gay Delavals, you would more than likely have found your stay punctuated with acts of mischief and moments of playfulness. Now, through the *Curtain Rises* project, you will see the property begin once again to live up to its outrageous reputation.

Don't worry. You won't find yourself falling prey to any of the crueler tricks that the Delavals are said to have played. There will be no unexpected dips in the pond and no false walls being raised to reveal you in a state of partial undress.

Instead you will come across all sorts of gentle surprises: hidden peepholes, objects that move, mirrors that distort and deceive, the sound of laughter and music and footsteps. The fire of 1822 may have robbed us of the original rooms and furnishings that played host to so many long nights of music, dancing, feasting and gambling, but the roguish spirit of Seaton Delaval Hall is returning and it's back to its old tricks.

Right, below Among the papers belonging to the Delavals there were found some playing cards – one of the pastimes that saw the family and their guests still placing wagers as the sun rose on their parties. On the blank reverse of some of these cards were notes written to friends – early examples of what became known as visiting cards in upper-class Georgian society

Right, above It is worth looking out for elements of playfulness built into the fabric of the hall itself. It is easy, for example, to imagine the Delavals taking great delight in revealing the door hidden in the wood panels of the Mahogany Parlour

Industry and trade

Next to the rounded bastion that marks the south-east corner of the pleasure grounds at Seaton Delaval Hall it is possible to make out the remains of a drawbridge. It originally spanned the ditch of the ha-ha so that the Delaval family and their guests could enjoy a walk to the harbour at Seaton Sluice.

That such a path exists between hall and harbour is no surprise, since the production and shipping of coal, salt and glass formed the foundation of the family's economic fortunes. It is fitting then that the *Curtain Rises* team decided to pick up on this part of the family's story in the foundations of the hall itself – by incorporating various references to industry in the basement chambers where once the servants of the house went about their duties.

Another reminder of the hall's industrial links can be found next to the site of the old drawbridge – in the 'clinker' that tops the adjoining wall. A waste product of the coal and glass industries, clinker is a dark stony residue with an impermeability that made it useful as a way of protecting walls from the elements.

The fact that the village of Hartley Pans was renamed Seaton Sluice pays tribute to the ingenuity of Sir Ralph Delaval, who devised a system of sluice gates in around 1670 to flush troublesome silt out of its harbour.

Sir John Delaval too had a taste for engineering works, and his younger brother Thomas had the technical and business acumen to launch the Royal Northumberland Bottle Works. For all that they were active players in the Gay Delaval generation, both John and Thomas had substance to go with their style – unlike their wastrel older brother Francis.

Of all the siblings in the Gay Delaval generation, it was Edward Delaval who perhaps lived a life furthest removed from the rest of the family – and one that linked the Delaval name to the very cutting edge of science and invention. A fellow of Pembroke College, Cambridge, Edward's wide-ranging academic interests saw him appointed alongside fellow polymath Benjamin Franklin, inventor of the lightning rod, to explore ways to protect St Paul's Cathedral in London from electrical storm damage. It was a subject on which he contributed papers to the Royal Society – alongside others relating to the field of optics. Especially well regarded for the precision of his experiments, Edward lived a quiet life in a 'neat Gothic house' in Westminster. He is said to have had its interior formed with artificial stone to make the house fireproof – a typically prudent measure which was sadly never undertaken at the family home in Northumberland.

Right Edward Delaval (1729–1814), painted during his time at Pembroke College, Cambridge

Craftsmanship, art and collections

Much of the character of Seaton Delaval Hall has come to be defined by the great fire of 1822, the scars of which can still so clearly be seen in the Entrance Hall and Saloon. Very little remains of the furniture and works of art that once adorned these grand spaces and the bedrooms now missing altogether from the upper floors.

Today the vast majority of the furniture in the central block and West Wing comprises items brought from other properties by the Astleys to refurnish the hall. Unusually for a property of this significance, this allowed the *Curtain Rises* team a great deal of flexibility in deciding which items to display and where to position them.

Treasured survivors

Naturally the few items thought to pre-date the fire were earmarked for particularly prominent display. These include the mahogany plinths in the Entrance Hall, which by some miracle escaped the full force of the great fire, and a pair of parcel-gilt pier tables, which appear to match

Above Rhoda Delaval, later Lady Astley (1725–57) by Arthur Pond, 1750

Right Parcel-gilt pier table, one of a pair, thought to be one of the few items in the collection dating from before the great fire items listed in an earlier inventory of the property, and which are similar in style to tables depicted in the background of a portrait at another of the family's properties at Doddington Hall.

Other items of particular significance are the portraits of various Delavals painted by local artist William Bell. A regular visitor to the hall – and for a time on the family's payroll – Bell produced many fine paintings of John, his wife Susannah and their children.

Creative company

The Delavals were more than simply patrons of the arts; they actively sought out the company of creative people and produced works of their own. Actors, authors, playwrights and painters – the Delavals counted many within their immediate social circle. One was artist Arthur Pond, who produced wonderful architectural paintings of the hall and some handsome portraits of the family, which still form part of the property's collection. It was Pond too who taught Rhoda Delaval, eldest of the Gay Delaval siblings, how to paint.

Rhoda went on to become an accomplished artist in her own right, producing excellent portraits in pastels of her brothers and sisters. It was a talent she pursued at Seaton Delaval Hall itself, where she kept house for her mother and father, and later lived with her husband, Edward Astley, heir to the baronetcy of Melton Constable. It was from this Norfolk estate that much of the collection now at Seaton Delaval Hall was brought in the 20th century, including some of Rhoda's own paintings, now back in the hall that their creator called home.

Open access

Although the team working on the *Curtain Rises* project had some freedom in choosing whether to display each piece in the collection, they did not want items to lie beyond the eyes of the public. Instead they decided to create an open

collection store in the West Wing to house and display items that were not chosen to appear in the other rooms. It is designed to be a fascinating space to explore – shining a well-deserved spotlight on what in the past would have been hidden away behind the scenes.

Above Sophia Anne Delaval, later Jadis (1755–95), daughter of John and Susannah, by local artist William Bell, 1770

Glorious grounds and gardens

Quite how much involvement Sir John Vanbrugh had in the design and construction of the grounds at Seaton Delaval Hall is unclear. It is known that some landscaping work had already been carried out before he was commissioned and that much of it was only completed after his death. It also appears that the work was not carried out according to one unifying design, but in a slightly less coherent fashion – with nods to the principles of Vanbrugh but also subject to the views of the family and shaped by the constraints and opportunities afforded by the gardens that had already been cultivated on the site for at least a century.

In the time of the Gay Delavals, guests would have arrived in the relatively austere surroundings of the forecourt and then been shown through the hall and out onto the South Portico. There they would have been greeted by a much more pastoral scene – just as you are today.

Within the boundaries of the four corner bastions sit the pleasure grounds, the South Lawn stretching invitingly out ahead bordered by carefully conceived areas of woodland to east and west. The eye is drawn along the line of the lawn to the monumental obelisk situated about half a mile away, and beyond to the ruins of Tynemouth Priory.

Strolling around the grounds would have revealed other features designed to catch the eye at just the right moment – the dramatic statues mounted on the corner bastions perhaps

or the artful unveiling of the Oval – a secluded lawn cut into the woodland to the south-east.

Venturing into the wider estate, guests might have strolled to the obelisk, taking in (and perhaps even dipping into) the large stone brick-lined Egg Pond along the way. Another path that eventually drops down to the harbour at Seaton Sluice leads past the Mausoleum erected in the late 1770s by Sir John Delaval as a memorial to his son Jack, who died at the age of 19. Never consecrated, possibly due to a row with the church authorities, it now stands in eerie abandonment.

New surprises

The designed landscape at Seaton Delaval Hall was most obviously shaped by the work undertaken throughout the 18th century, but the grounds have evolved and changed several times over the years. This remained true in the 20th century when Colonel Pollard and his family reinstated the Rose Garden with further developments made under the direction of Lord and Lady Hastings. As part of the *Curtain Rises* project, it was decided to reimagine the landscape by referring back to a surviving 1781 plan of the gardens and subterranean evidence picked up by a light detection and ranging (LiDAR) scan of the site.

Above **William Hardie of Studio Hardie, in the North-West Woodland**

The *Curtain Rises* project also intended that visitors should find brand new delights to discover – designed and installed by William Hardie of Studio Hardie. Here William, well known for his television work on Channel 4's Amazing Spaces and Shed of the Year, explains the thinking behind the new additions.

Tell us about the inspiration for your work at Seaton Delaval Hall

It's all about reanimating the spirit of the Delavals themselves – their flamboyance, their love of trickery, and especially their passion for Baroque theatre. When you look at Baroque theatres that survive today, the effects they achieve are simply mesmerising. There's a kind of magic to the way they use mechanical movement, illusion, false perspective and scene changes to make something so real and so dramatic. It's not the computer-generated imagery of Hollywood; it's real, physical illusion and it's all the better for it.

How have you translated that to the grounds here?

We have designed two interventions – one in the North-West Woodland and another in the woodland to the south-east. The first is a play area inspired by the elaborate candle-lit shows that the Delavals used to put on in the grounds. It's a space where children – and grown-ups – can play in a kind of magical theatrical world, with stages and pulleys and wheels and all of those behind-the-scenes mechanisms. That's something I really care about: letting people see the workings behind a design.

What about the second intervention?

Well, it's really a group of interventions – all in the south-east corner of the grounds. They play on the way that the gardens were originally designed to conceal and reveal various views and features. There was a gentle mischief and fun involved that we wanted to recapture. A kind of illusion. I don't want to say too much more so that visitors can enjoy discovering them for themselves, but it's fair to say that you can't always trust the evidence of your eyes!

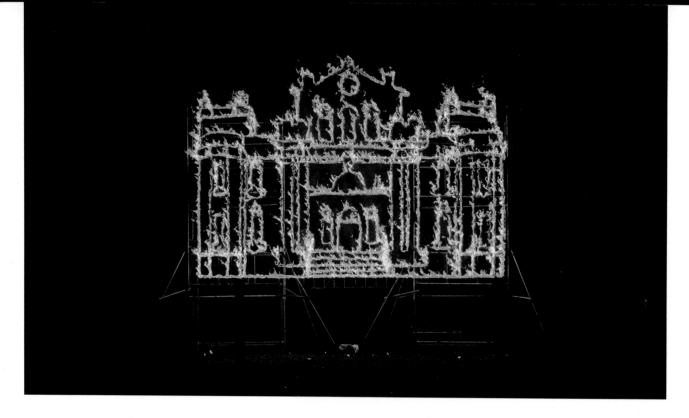

The Drama Continues

Seaton Delaval Hall is a survivor, its roots reaching back almost a millennium to the days of William the Conqueror.

Its story is one of continual change. Where once there stood a castle, a mansion was raised, and where once a mansion, an imposing hall. Trees were felled and planted and felled again. Gardens bloomed and withered; paths were laid and lost.

In time the rising winds of trade blew tall ships across the bay, laden with the Delaval riches of salt and coal and glass. Industries boomed and dwindled; fortunes were made, inherited and squandered; parties thrown and reputations forged.

Flames brought ruin, and a new century brought war. Then through the vision, labour and devotion of the estate's final family custodians the doors to the hall were thrown open, the public came and this extraordinary Northumbrian home came to assume the mantle of a national treasure.

Now the curtain rises on the latest – but by no means last – scene in the hall's proud tale. A scene of new surprises and delights, of fresh playfulness and enduring wonder.

The story continues. Seaton Delaval Hall lives on.

Above Fire drawing of Seaton Delaval Hall, created by students of Northumbria University in collaboration with Walk the Plank, November 2017